The Gift of Years

Bible reflections for older people

Contents

The Gift of Years: Bible reflections for older people © BRF 2014

Published by
The Bible Reading Fellowship
15 The Chambers, Vineyard,
Abingdon, OX14 3FE
United Kingdom
Tel: +44 (0)1865 319700
Email: enquiries@brf.org.uk
Website: www.brf.org.uk
BRF is a Registered Charity

ISBN 978 0 85746 413 2

First published 2014
10 9 8 7 6 5 4 3 2 1 0

Acknowledgements
Scripture quotations marked NIV are taken from the Holy Bible, New International Version, Anglicised edition, copyright © 1979, 1984, 2011 by Biblica (formerly International Bible Society). Used by permission of Hodder & Stoughton Publishers, an Hachette UK company. All rights reserved. 'NIV' is a registered trademark of Biblica (formerly International Bible Society). UK trademark number 1448790.

Scripture quotations marked NRSV are taken from the New Revised Standard Version of the Bible, Anglicised Edition, copyright © 1989, 1995 by the Division of Christian Education of the National Council of the Churches of Christ in the USA. Used by permission. All rights reserved.

Scripture quotations marked NLT are taken from the Holy Bible, New Living Translation, copyright © 1996, 2004. Used by permission of Tyndale House Publishers, Inc., Wheaton, Illinois 60189. All rights reserved.

Extracts from the Authorised Version of the Bible (The King James Bible), the rights in which are vested in the Crown, are reproduced by permission of the Crown's Patentee, Cambridge University Press.

Cover design and internal layout by Heather Knight

A catalogue record for this book is available from the British Library

Printed in the UK by Rainbow Print

From the Editor...

'Tricia
Williams

Welcome! We hope you will find these Bible reflections helpful and encouraging. Both of our writers, David Winter and Lin Ball, know for themselves, or through loved ones, the challenges (and joys!) of growing older.

David writes the series **Hope is the Promise**, reminding us of the certain hope of life with God: 'God is our refuge' (Psalm 62:8, NIV). In her series **Of Life and Loss**, Lin reflects on how as Christians we can bear the inevitable sense of loss that affects our lives as we grow older. We're reminded of God's promise: 'Even to your old age... I... will sustain you' (Isaiah 46:4, NIV).

We'd love to hear from you about how these reflections have helped you (see pp 31–32). Our prayer for this booklet is that, as you spend time with God, you will come closer to him, as he draws near to you.

God bless you,

'Tricia Williams

About the writers

David Winter is a former producer and Head of Religious Broadcasting at the BBC. He is also the author of 43 books, the most recent being *At the End of the Day: Enjoying Life in the Departure Lounge* (BRF). Now retired from full-time ministry, he lives in Berkshire.

Lin Ball's career began in journalism over 40 years ago. She feels blessed to have explored many different areas of writing. Highlights include interviewing missionaries for OMF, editing Bible resources with Scripture Union for over twelve years, and creating radio programmes about disability.

How to use *The Gift of Years* Bible reflections

Perhaps you have always had a special daily time for reading the Bible and praying. But now, as you grow older, you are finding it more difficult to keep to a regular pattern or find it hard to concentrate. Or, maybe you've never done this before. Whatever your situation, these Bible reflections aim to help you take a few moments to read God's word and pray, whenever you have time or feel that would be helpful.

Time with God

You may find it helpful to use these Bible reflections in the morning or last thing at night, or any time during the day. You could use them, as Debbie suggests in her welcome, as a way of making 'an appointment to chat with God'.

There are 20 daily Bible reflections here. Each one includes some verses from the Bible, a reflection to help you in your own thinking about God and a suggestion for prayer. The reflections aren't dated, so it doesn't matter if you don't want to read every day. The Bible verses are printed, but if you'd like to read from your own Bible that's fine too.

Using these reflections
• Take time to quieten yourself, becoming aware of God's presence, asking him to speak to you through the Bible and the reflection.
• Read the Bible verses and the reflection:
  - What do you especially like or find helpful in these verses?
  - What might God be saying to you through this reading?
  - Is there something to pray about or thank God for?
• Pray. Each reflection includes a prayer suggestion. You might like to pray for yourself or take the opportunity to think about and pray for others.

Hope is the promise

'Can you fix it?' I asked the plumber, as we both looked at a sink full of stagnant water. 'Mmm,' he said, 'I hope so.' It wasn't very reassuring, but a couple of hours and a good few pounds later the job was, in fact, done. 'Hope', in English, is a funny word, because we can use it to express real confidence, but also to convey an element of doubt. 'Have you passed your exams?' we ask a grandchild—and get the cautious reply, 'I hope so.'

When we come to the Bible, and especially the New Testament, the picture is quite different, because the writers aren't thinking of hope as a possibility, but as a promised certainty. Hope, for them, is trust in a God who keeps his word, and while the outcome may be long delayed, it is as certain as tomorrow's sunrise—a comparison made very beautifully in Psalm 130 (v. 6): 'My soul waits for the Lord more than those who watch for the morning' (NRSV).

Hope, for the New Testament writers, is not a vague emotion, a sort of optimistic feeling that something good might turn up, like Billy Bunter's postal order. Hope is a gift of God, one of those three things which, as St Paul said, 'abide' for ever, along with faith and love (1 Corinthians 13:13, NRSV). With God the eventual outcome will be good—indeed, glorious. That's hope, and it's a promise.

Psalm 33:18–22 (NRSV)

Steadfast love

Truly the eye of the Lord is on those who fear him, on those who hope in his steadfast love... Our soul waits for the Lord; he is our help and shield. Our heart is glad in him, because we trust in his holy name. Let your steadfast love, O Lord, be upon us, even as we hope in you.

When I meet a couple who are thinking of getting married, I often ask what each is bringing to the relationship, and what they expect to get from it. This psalm sets out precisely those two 'sides' of our relationship with God. He brings wonderful blessings to the relationship. His 'eye' will watch over us. He will help us and shield us from harm. Above all, his 'steadfast love' will be upon us. That's not a bad list!

However, on our side there are things we should bring to the relationship. We are to 'fear' him (the word simply means treat him with reverence, not take him lightly). We are to 'wait' for him, patiently trusting in what he has promised. Our hearts are to be 'glad' in him— this is a God who wants his people to be joyful. And above all, we are to find our 'hope' in his 'steadfast love'.

'Steadfast love' is a frequent phrase in the Psalms—it occurs 119 times! It is, it seems, the key quality of God's nature. However much we change, he doesn't. His love for us is 'steadfast'. So to put our trust and hope in 'the Lord' is to place our own ever-changing, fragile lives into the hands of a steadfast, unchanging and loving God.

Prayer
May I know in my life the 'steadfast love' of God, and, in praying and caring, share its blessing with those around me. Amen

Psalm 62:5–8 (NRSV)

God alone is my rock

For God alone my soul waits in silence, for my hope is from him. He alone is my rock and my salvation, my fortress; I shall not be shaken. On God rests my deliverance and my honour; my mighty rock, my refuge is in God. Trust in him at all times, O people; pour out your heart before him; God is a refuge for us.

Waiting isn't something most of us are good at, whether it's the bus that's late, the train that doesn't come, or a visit from friends and family we've been looking forward to for a while. We're constantly told in the Psalms (the hymn book of the Jews in Bible times) that we should 'wait on the Lord', but that's a different sort of 'waiting'. More like the waiter in a restaurant, we are to be ready and waiting to respond to God's prompting—perhaps to act generously, or to say 'sorry', or to offer help where it's needed.

When, in that sense of the word, we 'wait' on God, all kinds of good things can follow. In the silence of prayer he gives us hope. In times of trouble he holds us fast and offers us a 'refuge', a place of safety. When we feel we're nobodies, he gives us self-respect ('honour'). When nothing seems certain or secure, he alone is a 'rock' to which we can cling.

Prayer
As I silently wait to hear your voice, Lord, show me the sort of person you want me to be. Help me not just to cling to the rock myself, but to be a rock for others. Amen

Romans 12:9–13 (NRSV)

Genuine love

Let love be genuine; hate what is evil, hold fast to what is good; love one another with mutual affection; outdo one another in showing honour. Do not lag in zeal, be ardent in spirit, serve the Lord. Rejoice in hope, be patient in suffering, persevere in prayer. Contribute to the needs of the saints; extend hospitality to strangers.

'I love you,' he says, gazing into her eyes. But she, being a wise young woman, asks herself, 'Does he really mean it?' 'Let love be genuine,' says the apostle Paul, and then proceeds to offer a remarkably practical guide, starting with hating evil but 'holding fast' to what is good. Genuine love shows genuine affection, and draws it out of others—it's 'mutual'. It doesn't just talk the talk, but shows itself in action. It respects other people ('showing honour') and it has practical consequences—'contributing to the needs' of God's people and being hospitable: don't forget the 'food bank', or that neighbour who'll be alone at Christmas.

These practical signs of genuine love flow, we may note, from a loving heart. Those who show genuine love are full of hope themselves. They are 'patient in suffering'; they 'persevere in prayer'. It's not that they're 'do-gooders', but that the love of God in their hearts simply overflows into the lives of those around them. They don't need to preach. Their lives do the talking.

Prayer
Lord, create in me a heart of love—a love that reflects the love of Christ, who fed the hungry, cared for the poor and healed the sick. Amen

1 Corinthians 13:11–13 (NRSV)

Faith, hope and love

When I was a child, I spoke like a child, I thought like a child, I reasoned like a child; when I became an adult, I put an end to childish ways. For now we see in a mirror, dimly, but then we will see face to face. Now I know only in part; then I will know fully, even as I have been fully known. And now faith, hope, and love abide, these three; and the greatest of these is love.

This is a 'now and then' argument by the apostle Paul. Now, in the limitations of present experience, faith and hope are vital. We need faith to believe that there is a purpose in life, a loving Creator who cares about us. We need hope to believe that in the end all will be well, because God has prepared good things for those who love him. So one day we won't need faith (because we shall see for ourselves) or hope (because our hopes will have been fulfilled). But love— genuine love, as we were thinking in yesterday's reading—will be our constant experience, because, as the Bible says, 'God is love' (1 John 4:16). Love is the very air of heaven.

You may be familiar with this verse from the old hymn 'Gracious Spirit, Holy Ghost':

Faith will vanish into sight; / Hope be emptied in delight; / Love in heaven will shine more bright; / Therefore, give us Love.

(Christopher Wordsworth, 1862)

Prayer
May the love of God so dwell in me that it touches the lives of those I meet every day with faith and hope. And from that faith and hope, may love grow and flourish. Amen

Colossians 1:25–27 (NRSV)

The hope of glory

I became [the Church's] servant according to God's commission that was given to me for you, to make the word of God fully known, the mystery that has been hidden throughout the ages and generations but has now been revealed to his saints. To them God chose to make known how great among the Gentiles are the riches of the glory of this mystery, which is Christ in you, the hope of glory.

Ah, a mystery! They intrigue all of us—things that we can't explain, strange events which we've never understood, crimes that need Hercule Poirot to solve them!

Here the apostle Paul is using the word 'mystery' in a very particular way. A 'mystery', in the language of the first century, was not so much something you didn't understand as something that needed to be revealed. In order to understand a mystery some special clue or interpretation was required. The mystery he is talking about, he tells us, is 'the riches' of God's glory—a mystery that has been hidden throughout the ages but now, at last, is to be revealed to them.

I imagine the Christians at Colossae listening to Paul's letter when it was first read out, waiting to discover what the mystery was. When the disclosure came, it was simply this: 'Christ in you'. The presence of the living Jesus among them and in their hearts was the great hidden mystery, the 'hope of glory'!

Prayer
Lord, help me know the presence of Jesus in my life and to share this wonderful 'mystery' with others, so that they too can enjoy its riches. Amen

1 Thessalonians 4:15–18 (NRSV)

Together for ever

For this we declare to you by the word of the Lord, that we who are alive, who are left until the coming of the Lord, will by no means precede those who have died. For the Lord himself... will descend from heaven, and the dead in Christ will rise first. Then we who are alive, who are left, will be caught up in the clouds together with them to meet the Lord in the air; and so we will be with the Lord for ever. Therefore encourage one another with these words.

One of the inescapable facts about getting older is that one by one we lose people who were important to us. Old friends die, and so do partners and others who have been part of our daily lives. Naturally, this makes us wonder. What has happened to them? Shall we ever see them again? What does the 'resurrection of the dead' really mean when applied to actual people we've known and loved?

It was a question St Paul dealt with in this letter to the Christians at Thessalonica, probably written not much more than 20 years after the resurrection of Jesus. Christians then expected Jesus to return very soon—but what about those of their friends and family who had died in the meantime? His answer is clear. Christians who have already died will rise first, and then those who are still alive at his coming (whenever that is) will be 'caught up' together with them, and so we 'will be with the Lord for ever'. The key words are 'together' and 'for ever'. That's it, really!

Prayer
May this wonderful promise encourage me in my own faith, and also prompt me to encourage others who may be wondering about those they have loved and lost. Amen

Hebrews 6:17–19 (NRSV)

An anchor of the soul

In the same way, when God desired to show even more clearly to the heirs of the promise the unchangeable character of his purpose, he guaranteed it by an oath, so that through two unchangeable things, in which it is impossible that God would prove false, we who have taken refuge might be strongly encouraged to seize the hope set before us. We have this hope, a sure and steadfast anchor of the soul...

If someone we know and respect makes us a promise, backed up by a solemn oath, we can be sure that it will be fulfilled. Here, it says, God has promised two unchangeable things—that the whole world will be blessed through a descendant of Abraham, and that Jesus as our great High Priest is the means of our forgiveness (see Hebrews 6:13–14 and 7:25). God has sealed these promises with his own solemn oath. All we have to do is 'seize' it. What more could we ask?

Because we know and respect God, we can be confident that he will fulfil what he has promised. It's that confidence which is 'a sure and steadfast anchor of the soul'. Instead of drifting through life, blown here and there by the wind and at the mercy of every passing storm, we are held secure by that 'anchor' of the soul. The wind of change may blow and the storms of life's events may threaten us, but God's solemn promise is our security and hope...

Prayer
Lord, when I'm in danger of feeling that I've lost control of things, caught in the winds and storms of life, remind me of that 'anchor of the soul' which you have promised. Amen

An imperishable inheritance

Blessed be the God and Father of our Lord Jesus Christ! By his great mercy he has given us a new birth into a living hope through the resurrection of Jesus Christ from the dead, and into an inheritance that is imperishable, undefiled, and unfading, kept in heaven for you, who are being protected by the power of God through faith for a salvation ready to be revealed in the last time.

There are, as we all learnt at school, three tenses: past, present and future. All three are in this lovely opening to the first letter of Peter. He begins in the past. God has given us new birth into a new life through the resurrection of Jesus Christ. The key to that is our faith in Jesus and the badge of it was our baptism. That has happened, and it settles where we are now.

So that brings us to the present. We have been 'born' into a 'living hope'—that's to say, it's real and alive, not something in some dusty register. This hope is our inheritance—something willed by God, 'imperishable' (no sell-by date!) and unfading (it will remain bright and beautiful).

And so to the future. This inheritance, like a 'last will and testament', is safely stored away in the vaults of heaven, protected by the 'power of God' and waiting to be brought out 'in the last time'. There it is: past, present, future—all in God's safe hands.

Prayer
I don't know what the future holds, but I know who holds the future. May the God who touched my life hold me safe, keep me in his care, and bring me to his heavenly kingdom. Amen

The answer to anxiety

Do not worry about anything, but in everything by prayer and supplication with thanksgiving let your requests be made known to God. And the peace of God, which surpasses all understanding, will guard your hearts and your minds in Christ Jesus.

'Don't worry' is a common piece of advice, and generally quite unhelpful! We are worried, and what we want is an answer, not advice to stop worrying. As with similar advice from Jesus in the Sermon on the Mount (Matthew 6:34), an answer is offered here—it follows the very important word 'but'. Don't worry, but 'let your requests be made known to God'. I love the way that's worded—let them, don't stop them—bring the God who loves you into the situation that is causing your worry.

This is not simply a call to 'stop worrying', but a straightforward and practical answer. The process of 'letting God in on the problem' involves 'prayer', 'supplication' (literally, asking humbly) and (importantly) 'thanksgiving'. Often in our worries we forget all the things there are to be grateful for.

And then? The 'peace of God' will 'guard' our minds. The word the apostle used relates to a garrison guarding a city! Quite a promise.

Prayer
Lord, help me to meet the worries and anxieties of the day with the antidote of prayer, gratitude and faith, so that my life—and the lives of those for whom I pray—may be guarded from fear and lived out in peace. Amen

Matthew 11:28–30 (NRSV)

Good news for the weary

[Jesus said], 'Come to me, all you that are weary and are carrying heavy burdens, and I will give you rest. Take my yoke upon you, and learn from me; for I am gentle and humble in heart, and you will find rest for your souls. For my yoke is easy, and my burden is light.'

I can remember (just) when I never felt 'weary' and nothing much seemed a 'burden'. But the days come for all of us when even ordinary routine things—the shopping, the washing, cutting the grass in the garden—which we used to enjoy doing, gradually become 'burdens'. It's not just age (though that's part of it), but also the feeling that they must be done. They lie across our paths like obstacles to be overcome.

And they are the little burdens! What about living with a debilitating condition, or caring for a loved one who needs constant attention? There is an emotional 'weariness', too, often the product of loneliness.

So this invitation of Jesus springs off the pages of the Gospel as a glorious promise of hope. 'Come to me!' he says. What simpler invitation can there be? 'I will give you rest, share your burden, and teach you a better way.' We no longer need to feel that the burden is too heavy or the weariness overwhelming. 'Come to me!'

Prayer
Lord, sometimes I am weary, and sometimes there are burdens that I find I simply can't carry. As I accept your invitation and come to you with them, may I find 'rest for my soul'. Amen

The Gift of Years

Debbie Thrower

Meet Debbie...

Debbie Thrower is Team Leader of BRF's The Gift of Years ministry and is also an Anna Chaplain. Karen Laister, BRF's Deputy Chief Executive, talked to Debbie about her life, faith and ministry.

When did you become a Christian?

Growing up in a Christian family, as the youngest of three sisters, we went to church most Sundays. I remember always having a strong sense of God, of 'Someone' benign watching over me. Early childhood was spent in Africa, then, when I was six we moved to a remote but beautiful part of East Devon. Later I went to a Methodist boarding school which I realise now gave me a firm grounding in the Christian faith. In my 20s I became distracted by other things: university, a year teaching in France, starting work as a journalist. I still went to church sometimes, but my faith dwindled.

What prompted you to take up a ministry?

I was away from home making a programme with a BBC work colleague who was a Christian. Over supper one evening she started telling me about her faith. Later, I had a sleepless night thinking about how far I had strayed from my Christian roots. If Christianity was true, then didn't it demand my all? So began a journey of discovery. Once our children were teenagers, I offered myself for selection as a lay minister, a Reader, in the Church of England.

What led you into a ministry supporting older people?

I had seen what a difficult time older age was for my parents—all the physical, emotional and spiritual ups and downs. Some years later I saw a role of Chaplain to Older People advertised locally. At once I thought 'that is exactly what my parents could have done with'. My next thought was: 'You don't want me to do this, do you?!'

What makes you sad when you visit people?

For many, older age is blighted by loneliness, thoughts of inadequacy and futility. The 'what if's', the recriminations, the sorrows can plague us. Having an empathetic listener can help steer people away from destructive thoughts, reflect on forgiveness, and what they can look back on with gratitude. Such reflection can, curiously enough, foster hope and resilience for the future.

What thrills you about The Gift of Years ministry?

What excites me is that it takes the spiritual life of older people seriously. It is built on the premise that life is a gift, and that long life is a blessing, but it doesn't underestimate the challenges of this. I hope The Gift of Years will help people of all ages cherish the contribution of older people and discover that later life is something to embrace, rather than fear, as: '… we all, with open face beholding as in a glass the glory of the Lord, are changed into the same image from glory to glory…' (2 Corinthians 3:18, KJV).

Introduction

Of life and loss

'When I am an old woman,' Jenny Joseph (1961) mischievously writes in her poem 'Warning', 'I shall wear purple' with a red hat which doesn't match! She playfully imagines herself in older age, loosed from convention, free to do as she pleases. She will spend money with abandon on 'summer gloves and satin sandals'!

Perhaps less well known is T.S. Eliot's picture of an older man in 'The Love Song of J. Alfred Prufrock' (1915). He reflects on how he would part his thinning hair and whether to wear the bottoms of his trousers rolled whilst walking along the beach. His poem, though, is nothing like as playful as Joseph's. He laments lost opportunities and lack of spiritual progress in a life 'measured out… with coffee spoons.' Redundant. Side-lined from the action. A desperately sad picture. Is that how you see later life? Will you be full of regrets? Or will you celebrate your advancing years in outrageous purple and red?

My mum, now in her mid-80s and with early dementia, often remarks, 'Old age doesn't come alone.' No, it brings things that are unwelcome; robs us of things we would rather keep. So, how does the Christian bear with the loss?

Philippians 3:7–10 (NIV)

Priceless!

But whatever were gains to me I now consider loss for the sake of Christ. What is more, I consider everything a loss because of the surpassing worth of knowing Christ Jesus my Lord, for whose sake I have lost all things... I want to know Christ—yes, to know the power of his resurrection and participation in his sufferings, becoming like him in his death...

Taking stock comes with the territory of advancing years. And it can be sobering to attempt to assess the outcomes of a life. There's career, family, hobbies, friends, church life. At best, they add up to personal fulfilment. At worst, they fall worryingly short of a life well lived; or even a life without regrets. Not many of us can lay claim to a life that's more than ordinary.

It's easy to fall into the trap of comparing ourselves against the perspective paraded by contemporary media. Thankfully, the Christian is weighed in a different set of measuring scales. 'Yes, everything else is worthless when compared with the infinite value of knowing Christ Jesus my Lord' is the New Living Translation's take on the first verse of today's reading. If you know Christ as your Lord, Master and companion, you possess the most valuable treasure imaginable. Anything sacrificed for the cause of Christ—a loss in the world's estimation—can be a gain in disguise!

Prayer
How beyond price is the salvation you have given me, Father! Help me today to cherish it; to hold a truer estimation of its worth. And give me a desire humbly to share that perspective, that others may see how empty the search is after the dreams of this world. Amen

Psalm 25:5–7, 10 (NIV)

Love me tender

Guide me in your truth and teach me, for you are God my Saviour, and my hope is in you all day long. Remember, Lord, your great mercy and love, for they are from of old. Do not remember the sins of my youth and my rebellious ways; according to your love remember me, for you, Lord, are good... All the ways of the Lord are loving and faithful...

Were you an Elvis Presley fan? He was considered daring in his day, yet his lyrics and stage performances were naïve compared to those of today's chart toppers. His 'Love Me Tender' got a million advance orders the day after he sang it on TV in 1956—a gold record before it was even released.

Today the popularity of songs is measured in downloads or tweets. It's a different world. Intriguingly, the favoured topic remains the same as in our youth. Love. We all want to love and to be loved. But in later life we may find we have lost the love and companionship that was dearest to us.

In this psalm, as in so many, the writer's returning theme is God's unfailing love for us (v. 10). His is the greatest love of all, and it will always be ours. It's a love that teaches us that the truth (v. 5) is compassionate, forgiving and merciful (v. 6–7), and feels our pain (v. 18). It's a love in which we can feel secure, no matter what life brings.

Prayer
'As Solomon grew old... his heart was not fully devoted to the Lord his God' (1 Kings 11:4, NIV). Father, give me the teachable heart of a child with the wisdom of age, always remembering that your love for me can never be lost. Amen

Psalm 92:12–15 (NIV)

Vital and green

The righteous will flourish like a palm tree, they will grow like a cedar of Lebanon; planted in the house of the Lord, they will flourish in the courts of our God. They will still bear fruit in old age, they will stay fresh and green, proclaiming, 'The Lord is upright; he is my Rock, and there is no wickedness in him.'

Driving through the Leicestershire countryside on a soft early summer's day, I saw my surroundings with new eyes. Sitting next to me was my friend Shirley, visiting from Canada. The grazing sheep, the timbered cottages with thatched roofs, even the poppies growing wild on the verge—all was a delight to her. We made many stops as Shirley snapped away with her camera.

What most enchanted me that day were the different greens of grass, trees and rolling pasture which somehow gladdened my eyes and lifted my heart. I found myself repeating snatches of this psalm, which sings of the desire to be fruitful, fresh, green and young in spirit even when the body inevitably passes from autumn to winter. 'Vital and green' (v.14) is how the New Living Translation puts it. How is it possible to 'still bear fruit in old age'? Checking my Bible, I see that the key to this flourishing is in being righteous—which, of course, is only possible by staying close to the God who forgives and makes clean.

Prayer
Tell God of your commitment to stay close to him through all life's seasons, and your desire to be fruitful for him. Read the psalm again, making it personal: 'I will flourish… I will grow… I will bear fruit… I will stay fresh and green… he is my Rock.'

Ecclesiastes 7:10–14 (NLT)

Flickering greatness

Don't long for 'the good old days.' This is not wise. Wisdom is even better when you have money. Both are a benefit as you go through life. Wisdom and money can get you almost anything, but only wisdom can save your life. Accept the way God does things, for who can straighten what he has made crooked? Enjoy prosperity while you can, but when hard times strike, realise that both come from God. Remember that nothing is certain in this life.

'If only' is one of the saddest phrases in the English language. While no one wants to be a doormat, just accepting the unexpected twists and turns of life with stoicism rather than regret can be a recipe for a calmer life. The threat of lessening independence or the fear of increasing irrelevance can make us regret the passing years. It's not just that as time passes we need a stronger prescription for our spectacles; perhaps we are inclined to wear them with an over-rosy tint! But that way lies bitterness about present losses and denial about the future.

As T.S. Eliot's wonderfully-named J. Alfred Prufrock says, the older man is past his best by society's reckoning: 'I have seen the eternal Footman… snicker,' and he adds, poignantly, he is afraid.

Life's losses and uncertainties may catch us out—but they are no surprise to God. Both the rough path and the smooth are part of his design. He can be trusted with my future—and yours.

Prayer
'God, grant me the serenity to accept the things I cannot change, the courage to change the things I can, and wisdom to know the difference.'
(Reinhold Niebuhr)

Acts 2:16–18 (NIV)

Our generous God

... this is what was spoken by the prophet Joel: 'In the last days, God says, I will pour out my Spirit on all people. Your sons and daughters will prophesy, your young men will see visions, your old men will dream dreams. Even on my servants, both men and women, I will pour out my Spirit in those days, and they will prophesy.'

It's all down to 'the power of counting your blessings' a headline in *The Daily Telegraph* announced (20 March 2014). The generation who lived through the World War II are apparently happier than younger people—despite challenges like failing health or isolation. Could it be that counting your blessings helps you learn contentment with your lot, even when life seems to be diminishing on several fronts?

Are you a 'glass half empty' or a 'glass half full' kind of person? I'm pretty sure that over the years I've made a subtle transfer from one to the other. I was a gloomy, cynical teenager in the swingin' 60s. But now I find myself more able to be positive, even cheerful! The secret is not so much the ability to count my blessings—though that's definitely something I try to do—but it's in the certainty I gain from the Bible that God is not ageist. He is as willing to bless the older person as the younger one. There is no need for any of us to lose our spiritual vitality as the years pass. As this glorious passage tells us, his Spirit is shared generously with all.

Prayer
Spend some time before God counting your blessings. Then ask him for a generous portion of his Spirit. Tell him that you are ready, with and through his Spirit, to be about his work in the world today. Pray for those you might interact with today.

2 Corinthians 4:15–17 (NIV)

Don't lose heart!

All this is for your benefit, so that the grace that is reaching more and more people may cause thanksgiving to overflow to the glory of God. Therefore we do not lose heart. Though outwardly we are wasting away, yet inwardly we are being renewed day by day. For our light and momentary troubles are achieving for us an eternal glory that far outweighs them all.

I was sitting in a quiet café in a country park when suddenly it was invaded by about 20 laughing and confident ladies of later years, all wearing purple outfits, plenty of bling and with the most amazing collection of red fascinators bouncing on their grey heads. I was witnessing a gathering of the British Red Hatters who are inspired by the Jenny Joseph poem, 'When I am old I shall wear purple' (see Introduction, p. 18)! These lively ladies were determined not to become invisible, but to live life to the full.

We have every reason not to lose heart, says Paul. Spiritually, losing heart is a by-product of losing sight. I lose heart when my eyes see no more than the physical, with all its irreversible signs of decay. But when I lift my eyes to see the eternal, to the glorious inheritance I have in Christ, then my true perspective is restored. And I reach into my wardrobe for my purple dancing shoes!

Prayer
Forgive me, Father, for fixing my eyes on what is fleeting. What stares back from the mirror is not all there is to me. Physically there is decay; inside I am renewed day by day. Praise God! Help me not to lose heart but live courageously, looking ahead without fear. Amen

Ephesians 4:32—5:2 (NIV)

As fragrant as a rose

Be kind and compassionate to one another, forgiving each other, just as in Christ God forgave you. Follow God's example, therefore, as dearly loved children and live a life of love, just as Christ loved us and gave himself up for us as a fragrant offering and sacrifice to God.

The *Daily Mail* has dubbed them 'the sandwich generation': people who have given up paid work in their 60s or 70s, who have older parents living and needing support—while at the same time they are regularly caring for grandchildren. If you are not one of 'the sandwich generation' then you will likely have friends who are. Life can be pressured at a time when you might reasonably have expected to take things a little easier, perhaps going travelling or doing more gardening.

Giving in this way can be costly. If you are physically running on empty, think how you might relieve some pressure. Some days when I have my lively grandchildren to stay, I meet up with another grandparent who's also caring for grandchildren. It's even noisier! But somehow sharing the day makes it easier. If you are spiritually running on empty, that too needs creative attention. What could you do? Join a prayer triplet? Go on a regular retreat? Create a 'sacred space' in your diary that's just for you and God?

But don't stop giving! In the end it's about living and loving as Christ has lived and loved. Not easy. But as fragrant as a rose.

Prayer
Name before God those you know who are weary with doing good, feeling they have lost their energy. Ask him to help them to do their caring from a place of feeling refreshed and restored—spiritually and physically.

1 Corinthians 15:40–44 (NIV)

Loss—and glory!

... the splendour of the heavenly bodies is one kind, and the splendour of the earthly bodies is another... So will it be with the resurrection of the dead. The body that is sown is perishable, it is raised imperishable; it is sown in dishonour, it is raised in glory; it is sown in weakness, it is raised in power; it is sown a natural body, it is raised a spiritual body.

Why is a meeting of over 60s like a musical event? Both can be 'organ recitals'! All too often when older people get together it's for an update on the latest aches and pains or comparing notes on medication!

It's good to empathise. But how much more encouraging when you can point your friends to the hope Christians have that's beyond the grave, when the mortal puts on immortality. Perhaps we recall the 'splendour' of our bodies of earlier years. But don't be too wistful about it! The ageing process takes us closer to a far more glorious state.

On the first anniversary of my father's death, my mother and us four siblings met in the crematorium. I gave each of them a packet of anemone seeds. How was it possible that these shrivelled black seeds when germinated in the ground would produce vibrant, beautiful flowers? It's a mystery! But the same miracle awaits all who believe in Jesus. 'Our bodies are buried in brokenness, but they will be raised in glory. They are buried in weakness, but they will be raised in strength' (v. 43, NLT). Praise God!

Prayer
Father, help me to share with others how they can know the assurance of the resurrection of the dead, so that they can live in eager expectation of that miracle in their own lives. Amen

Ephesians 4:29–32 (NIV)

Building up

Do not let any unwholesome talk come out of your mouths, but only what is helpful for building others up according to their needs... And do not grieve the Holy Spirit of God, with whom you were sealed for the day of redemption. Get rid of all bitterness, rage and anger, brawling and slander, along with every form of malice. Be kind and compassionate to one another, forgiving each other, just as in Christ God forgave you.

I confess that when I was young in the faith it seemed more important to me to share my opinions than to encourage consensus! Now I see how destructive and divisive this can be. I used to see older Christians as being prone to wishy-washy compromise. Now I know that kindness is one of the greatest virtues.

Often the viewing platform of youth is raised by unwarranted confidence. That's not a criticism; they don't know what they don't know! The viewing platform of age is lowered by the losses of the years: status, loved ones, health—they all take their toll. But somehow, the panorama that opens up before us is wider and higher. Experience, like God himself, both gives and takes away.

Since we've been seeking and receiving God's forgiveness over many years, the hope is that we know more about how to forgive others. If we all opened our mouths only to bless others and build them up, what a vibrant, Jesus-like community we would be!

Prayer
Dear God, cleanse my life of bitterness. Let the losses of life teach me kindness to others. May my conversation be wholesome and kind. And, however small I measure my influence to be, may I lead others in the way of kindness and forgiveness too. Amen

Isaiah 46:3–4 (NIV)

The God who sustains

'Listen to me, you descendants of Jacob, all the remnant of the people of Israel, you whom I have upheld since your birth, and have carried since you were born. Even to your old age and grey hairs I am he, I am he who will sustain you. I have made you and I will carry you; I will sustain you and I will rescue you.'

The fact of God knowing us from our mother's womb (Psalm 139:13–16) is often preached on—and it's a wonderful truth! But equally wonderful is God's promise to be with us and sustain us, however long our lives may be.

While the unborn baby is unspoilt and full of promise, the longer we live the more we become, like the man in the house that Jack built, 'all tattered and torn'. Yet still God's amazing love for us remains, despite our loss of innocence and failure to live up to all that was present in us in our youth.

The famous Baptist preacher Charles Haddon Spurgeon (1834–92), at the tender age of 22, preached on these verses—a sermon that's well worth reading. He had no doubt that a faithful God could sustain anyone, however long they lived, and pointed to the unfailing seasons of nature as confirmation. He said: 'Man's wine becomes dregs at the last, but God's wine is sweeter the deeper you drink of it.'

Prayer
Ask the God who sustains to reveal himself to anyone you know who is feeling anxious, insecure and vulnerable. Claim for yourself and for them the promise of Isaiah 46:4: 'I will be your God throughout your lifetime... I made you, and I will care for you...' (NLT)

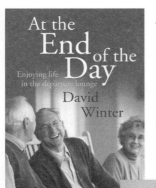

At the End of the Day

David Winter

ISBN: 978 0 85746 057 8

£6.99

David Winter writes:

I wrote At the End of the Day *because I wanted to address this situation not as a problem (which is how sociologists, politicians and media commentators seem to see it) but simply as yet another life experience. All through life we move more or less seamlessly from one stage to another, from childhood to adolescence, from that to young adulthood, from that to middle age, and from that to the retirement years. This book is an attempt to record what it is like finally to move into the departure lounge of life, awaiting the call to board our flight from this life to whatever it is that God has planned for us at its end.*

To order a copy of *At the End of the Day*, see page 32.

Keep in touch!

These undated Bible reading reflections are written to support those who are facing older age and the challenges and joys this brings. Developing and growing our relationship with God is important at every stage of life. However, as we grow older our faith and spiritual needs change: The Gift of Years is designed to offer support and encouragement in this stage of life.

We would love to hear what you think about these Bible reflections...
We are considering developing this booklet into a regular series. By completing the questionnaire on the opposite page (page 31), you will help us resource the needs of older people better.

Find out more...
You can receive The Gift of Years newsletter regularly to keep informed about developments and news from The Gift of Years. Complete the form on the following page to keep in touch.

To register your interest in receiving *The Gift of Years* Bible reflections regularly, complete your details on page 31.

Order more copies for your friends...
If you have enjoyed using these Bible reflections, you will find a form for ordering more copies on page 32. There is also a special offer for churches wanting to order packs of ten copies.

The Gift of Years is a new ministry, supported, resourced and enabled by BRF.

Visit www.thegiftofyears.org.uk to find out more.

We need your feedback!

Please complete this questionnaire, cut it out and send to the FREEPOST address at the bottom of this page.

1. I would like to see this being a regular series of Bible reading notes Yes/No (please circle)
2. Please rate how useful you have found the content and format of this booklet by circling the appropriate number (1 being not helpful and 5 being very helpful).

The content

Debbie's letter	1	2	3	4	5
About the writers	1	2	3	4	5
How to use the reflections	1	2	3	4	5
Meet Debbie	1	2	3	4	5
Hope is the Promise	1	2	3	4	5
Of Life and Loss	1	2	3	4	5
Information about other BRF resources	1	2	3	4	5

The booklet

Size and weight	1	2	3	4	5
Legibility and readability of text	1	2	3	4	5
Page layout	1	2	3	4	5
Cover design	1	2	3	4	5
Page design	1	2	3	4	5

3. Do you have any other comments? ....
....

Please cut out this page and return it to:
FREEPOST RRLH–JCYA–SZXR, TGOY Administrator, BRF, 15 The Chambers, Vineyard, Abingdon, OX14 3FE

Thank you!

To keep in touch, complete the following (please tick):

Yes, I would like to keep in touch with news about The Gift of Years. ☐

Yes, I would be interested in receiving *The Gift of Years* Bible reflections regularly. ☐

My address is: ....
....

My email address is: ....

How to order

Please quote TGOYBRN14 when placing your order.

- Visit **www.brfonline.org.uk**
- Telephone BRF Direct 01865 319700; Fax 01865 319701
- Email enquiries@brf.org.uk
- Complete the order form below and send it to:
  BRF, 15 The Chambers, Vineyard, Abingdon OX14 3FE

General Information

Delivery times within the UK are normally 15 working days
All prices are subject to the current rate of VAT
Prices are correct at the time of going to press
but may change without prior notice

The BRF office is open 9.15 am to 5.30 pm, Monday to Friday

Your local Christian bookshop will stock BRF titles

ISBN	TITLE	PRICE	QTY	TOTAL
978 0 85746 057 8	At the End of the Day	£6.99		
978 0 85746 242 8	Facing Illness, Finding Peace	£6.99		
978 0 85746 413 2	The Gift of Years Bible Reading Notes	£2.50		
978 0 85746 178 0	The Gift of Years Bible Reading Notes Pack of 10	£20.00		

Postage & Packing Charges				
Order value	UK	Europe	Surface	Air Mail
Under £7.00	£1.25	£3.00	£3.50	£5.50
£7.00–29.99	£2.25	£5.50	£6.50	£10.00
£30.00 and over	FREE	Prices on request		

Total value of books	
Postage and packing	
Donation	
Total for this order	

Please complete in BLOCK CAPITALS

Title.............. First name (or initial) .... Surname .... Acc. No. ....

Address ....

.... Postcode ....

Telephone .... Email ....

❏ Please email me details of BRF books, offers and news.

Method of payment

❏ Cheque ❏ MasterCard ❏ Visa ❏ Postal Order

Card no. ☐☐☐☐ ☐☐☐☐ ☐☐☐☐ ☐☐☐☐

*Last 3 digits on the reverse of the card
ESSENTIAL IN ORDER TO PROCESS
YOUR ORDER

Valid from ☐☐ ☐☐ Expires ☐☐ ☐☐ Security code* ☐☐☐

*1234 **567***
EXAMPLE

Signature .... Date .... /............... /...............
ESSENTIAL IF PAYING BY CREDIT CARD

All orders must be accompanied by the appropriate payment. Please make cheques payable to BRF.

Gift Aid Declaration

❏ I want BRF to claim back tax on this gift and any future gifts. I confirm I have paid or will pay an amount
of Income Tax and/or Capital Gains Tax for each tax year that is at least equal to the amount of tax that
all the charities that I donate to will reclaim on my gifts for that tax year.

❏ My donation does not qualify for Gift Aid.

Signature .... Date .... /............... /...............

Notes:
1. Please notify BRF if you want to cancel this declaration, change your name or home address, or no longer pay sufficient tax
on your income and/or capital gains.
2. If you pay Income Tax at the higher/additional rate and want to receive the additional tax relief due to you, you must include
all your Gift Aid donations on your Self-Assessment tax return or ask HM Revenue and Customs to adjust your tax code.

 www.facebook.com/biblereadingfellowship www.twitter.com/brfonline

PROMO REF: TGOYBRN1
BRF is a Registered Charity (23328